Through the
Eyes of the Soul

Through the Eyes of the Soul

Leona Byrne

Through the Eyes of the Soul

©2012 Leona Byrne

Published by Self Investment Publishing
2219 E. Thousand Oak Blvd.
Suite 102-386
Thousand Oaks, CA 91362

Cover Design © 2012 Michael Simpson

10 9 8 7 6 5 4 3 2 1

ISBN: 10: 0981523889
ISBN: 13: 978-0981523880

Introduction

In this book I share my poetry which captures my journey into that part of me which is Spirit. I believe I am not alone in this quest for Spiritual growth. Today many are seeking answers to what is the meaning of life and how to be happy in a world which seems to operate on judgment and blame. This judgment and blame causes pain and turmoil for many. I found that as I wrote, simple but beautiful lessons came to the surface and reflected what was going on in my mind, heart and soul. I wrote about my own experiences and what I learned from them. I felt inspired and when I shared these poems with others they seemed to be inspired too. I decided to put my poems in a book because I wanted others to understand and experience some of my learnings. The book contains my poetry and also the opportunity to develop and practice the spiritual concepts in each poem.

I have organized my book into five sections which cover different spiritual concepts. They are:

- Ego and Life Lessons
- Developing Awareness and Compassion
- Go Within
- Awe, Wonder, Gratitude
- Connection to all creation

Although there is some overlap in these areas the spiritual concepts which when contemplated and implemented lift the consciousness of individuals. Consciousness is what we see, hear, believe, think and how we relate to the world. It is our awareness of everything around us. When one person evolves spiritually all humanity moves forward.

How to use this book

During my process of enfolding awareness I was inspired to write poetry about my experiences and the lessons I learned. My writing reflects the thoughts and processes of what I observed from my higher self that is my Soul. I found that seeing life from the eyes of my soul transformed me. It is a practice I continue to strive to do daily. In this book I am sharing my heart and soul and hope that it inspires the reader to develop an awareness of their own Loving self. It is recommended that each poem be read and reflected on. The reflection pages are designed for reflection and an opportunity to carry the lessons learned into one's life. Don't rush through the book. Take a week or so on each poem if you can and see what changes and improvements occur in your life. You may prefer to use the book as a meditation guide and read a poem then meditate on it. I recommend that you journal your intentions and insights.

It is hoped that my sharing in this will touch your soul deeply and create healing that can be carried forward to the world's problems. I believe that love is the cure for the world's ills and it comes by healing one person at a time.

May Spirit guide you through your life's journey and may you know you are loved.

Contents

Section 1

Ego and Life Lessons

Section I
Ego and Life Lessons
Introduction

As children we experience things in our lives and we interpret these experiences. As a result certain beliefs form that end up later to limit our connection to Spirit. For example, a father leaves the home due to divorce or death and the child feels abandoned. A limiting belief forms such as "I am not worthy of love" or "I did something wrong and therefore I am not lovable".

The ego develops such limiting beliefs as a protection from what it perceives as hurt and disturbance. As a result life lessons that need healing pop up regularly during a person's life until a person figures out what the lesson is. We know there is a lesson to be learned when upset occurs during our life experiences. The ego tries to hold on to what it knows and often resists the learning.

Everyday life means dealing with upset in the form of anger, hurt, blame and feelings of inadequacy. This leads to suffering. The ego deals with this suffering by blaming others, resisting change, repeating bad choices, and projecting our own weaknesses onto others.

Until one takes a serious look at their feelings and limiting beliefs they cannot heal. Forgiveness and compassion and love will heal the belief. This takes courage. The way to know if an issue/limiting belief is healed is when there is no longer upset when the same thing that triggers the upset occurs. For example the child whose father left them will live out their limiting beliefs by having problems with relationships until they face and acknowledge their feelings of sadness.

Baby Roland

Beautiful little eyes see all so innocently.

Everything is new and wondrous to the child.

The world is his to claim and marvel at.

Nothing preconceived or set in stone like clay ready to mold.

Mysterious power is at hand if not unlearned.

The strength is in the appreciation of the joys of now.

His power can achieve holiness in a childhood state.

Reflections

A small child lives in the now but as he grows he forms judgments about his experience. These judgments create limiting beliefs which have a profound effect on one's life.

Can you think of a limiting belief that you have? (e.g. I am stupid. I must be careful, No one listens to me). Who besides yourself is involved in your limiting belief? For example your mother was impatient and brusque with you, resulting in the above examples of limiting beliefs.

Write down the limiting belief or beliefs then forgive yourself and any others involved in developing the belief or beliefs. The wording could be; "I forgive myself for buying into the belief that I am …..(stupid, inept, unworthy or whatever resonates with you). The truth is I am a worthwhile person doing the best I can.

Then forgive the person; for example "I forgive my mother for being abusive and I surrender this judgment to God."

Writing this helps to release the beliefs and allows you to form new beliefs that are more beneficial to you. It is recommended that you read what you wrote every day for a week.

Building a House of Peace

Peace is upstairs, I can find it there.

Downstairs is where I find I am right now,

amidst the clutter, confusion and pain,

How can I climb the stairs when I only

know this part of the house?

Follow the blueprint of love

and it becomes so much easier.

Forgiveness is the first step to take me up

and the burden lightens.

Acceptance is at the next level and the

clearing is amazing.

Down the hall there is compassion

for self and others as

I wonder what took so long

to find the way.

Ascension is not so hard if

you know where the steps are.

But until the way becomes clear and

one wants to comprehend,

shadow plays an elusive game

of hide and seek with the light.

Reflections

The key to loving and healing oneself is forgiveness, acceptance and compassion.

Is there someone in your life for which you still harbor a grudge? Can you be compassionate and forgive that person? Can you surrender into acceptance that what happened simply happened?

Write your thoughts and feelings on this.

Set an intention this week to forgive whenever you feel upset over what someone says or does.

Cover Up

So often we draw comfort in the excesses of food or drink.

It's easy to hide the pain and not look at ourselves.

Strangely enough under the pain lies the center of Beauty.

If only we knew how to get there.

How do we wake up and become aware?

But that's what life is all about...to learn the lesson.

Love lies within and is always there.

Reflections

When experiencing emotional or mental pain your ego tries to distract you by overeating, drinking excessively, or other obsessive behavior.

Do you eat or drink excessively when experiencing emotional or mental pain?

Acknowledge the pain then go within and find the loving inside.

Write about this and what do you do when feeling pain.

Make a conscious choice to go within when upset, stressed, uncomfortable, etc.

Distraction

The noise and clamour bangs out a beat.

It distracts and sends one down a different path.

One that allows you to look elsewhere but at yourself.

Keep the focus on the outside and

you won't know who you are.

What's so scary that you can't take a peek?

Uncover the pain and look at the root.

Only then will you know what is really there.

On the inside is the truth of your loving essence.

Find the keys of forgiveness, love and acceptance

to know yourself as the perfect peaceful being you are.

Reflections

The ego does not like change and will distract one from looking at oneself, from changing limiting beliefs and from taking responsibility for letting go of hurts.

These distractions can be loud music, smoking, taking on too many projects, overuse of the computer, too much television; anything that keeps you from coming into a state of peace and acceptance. When you become aware of what you are distracting yourself with you can make the changes that ego wants to hang onto.

How do you distract yourself from looking at yourself, going within and taking responsibility for letting go of hurts?

After reflecting on what you do to distract yourself and avoid going within make an intention every day this week to observe yourself and notice what you do to distract yourself.

Free

As I enfold into my beauty

I draw subliminal joy and energy to me.

Swirls of colored passion

entwine me in the bliss of peace.

Acceptance of what is... I have found

this to be the first profound lesson.

The one that opens the gateway

to the next lesson which is simply Love.

In the Loving I learn to understand

the connection of Spirit in us all.

Then comes the final Truth,

the lesson of forgiveness.

It is in forgiveness that

we blossom and are set free.

Free to be who we are;

Divine Essence in beautiful human form.

Reflections

Acceptance, letting go, Love and forgiveness of hurts frees us to open ourselves up to be who we truly are. When you are in the state of loving acceptance you will find that you are happier and more creative in expressing yourself.

How does it feel to be in a state of Loving acceptance?

For one week start your day by setting an intention to be in a state of Loving acceptance.

Notice how you feel and what changes occur in your life when you focus on loving acceptance.

Life Lessons

Life gives us the opportunity to learn our lessons.

Like an infant who stumbles taking its first steps

we fall into fear and frustration but try again and again.

It is our soul purpose to reach for the light.

Even though we may not know why, we toddle toward it

wondering what can make us happy

when all along the arms of God surround us,

enfold us, hold us from within.

We learn our lessons through the power of Love.

Reflections

When you experience upset it means that you are learning something. You are learning lessons such as *love is within* us and *happiness is our natural state* despite the bad things we experience.

When something is bothering you, do you look at what is really bothering you? Do you ignore your pain or do you blame others?

Make a conscious effort for a week or more to be aware of when you become upset.

Set your intention each morning to pay attention to what you feel and not react when upset.

Go inside and find the Peace and Loving that is the real you.

Not Your Burden

The assaults came as the ego hung on to old hurts.

Tremors felt far away and buried in the body.

To fester as emotional wounds manifest in physical pain.

Let go, let go spoke the little voice.

They are not your burden.

Tears and fears had locked in the suffering

for so long and familiar.

But time also brought the light as

Loving started to soothe.

Just apply the loving to the parts that hurt

and steep in the Divine.

Allow the change, fast or slow

to uncover the truth.

All levels will glow and transform

as outer and inner clear.

The perfection of you will emerge as

God's Divine reflection.

Reflections

This poem talks about how the ego hangs on to old hurts. Clinging to these upsetting old hurts not only creates continuing mental and emotional pain but this pain also affects the body. It is important to let go but first it is necessary to identify the old hurts and where they originated.

Acknowledge the pain by admitting that you feel sad, angry or whatever you feel. Don't bury your feelings but instead examine them and find out where the feelings come from and where they originated.

Ask yourself, what triggers bad feelings in me? Is this a common occurrence and does it have a common theme?

When feeling bad, stressed or angry do you have physical pain such as a back ache or headache as well?

Ask for Spirit's assistance then think about what upsets you and what triggers this upset. Write this down then go back and find the beginnings of these feelings. Do this by being silent and in a meditative state. Ask Spirit to assist you and guide you into understanding why you have upset. Surround yourself with love and release these upset feelings. It's O.K. to cry.

Spend time in the Loving and ask God for assistance in letting it go. When done burn the paper with the written hurts on it. Say a prayer; I release these hurts to God to be transformed into Love. I let go, let go, let go.

Projection

It's so easy to blame the other for our sins.

We don't have to look at ourselves.

It somehow eases the pain of our own misery.

When we face what's real and forgive ourselves

we can come to understand

the profound reality that we do the best we can.

That is life's purpose, to heal not to blame.

Letting go in Love is the shift that

can make us melt into our true nature.

Reflections

The ego does not like to look at what it perceives as our own weaknesses. You will find that when someone blames another and points out their faults that it is because they are afraid and ashamed to look at themselves. The truth is we are all learning our lessons and growing.

How did you feel when you blamed another?? Were you angry at their transgression or disgusted, etc.? Did this make you feel superior?

Take a look closely and see if there is something in yourself that you are ashamed of.

Forgive yourself for not being as perfect as you think you should be and practice being compassionate toward the one you blamed.

Do this by saying I forgive myself for judging myself as _____ or I forgive myself for not being perfect, the truth is I am doing the best I can.

Practice compassion by sending Love to the person you blamed.

This may take practice but if you let go of the upset and come into a state of peace and loving you can send love because you feel loving.

Spiderweb Patterns

Old patterns of unhappiness are like the

spiderwebs that stick to our daily activities.

They pull us back into old, useless

familiar patterns of thought and feeling.

Breaking free is painful but worthwhile.

The problem is that its so easy to stay put until

forced to wrench oneself out of the mesh.

Breaking free becomes the start of a

new design of creative life's expression.

It is then that the sun comes out

and the world is fresh and sparkly.

Reflections

The ego holds on to old patterns which may have been useful at one time. As a result we are unhappy, frustrated and fearful. To change old patterns, they must first be acknowledged and looked at.

Are you dealing with habitual habits of sadness and worry or other things such as fear or being overwhelmed? What triggers them?

Write these realizations down and then surrender them to God. Take time to be quiet and peaceful as you do this process.

Don't rush, let go when you are ready. You may review and let go of one habit at a time if this is easier and less overwhelming.

At this point you can burn the paper as a symbol of letting go of your old negative thoughts.

The New Path

I tread slowly afraid of what lies ahead.

Yet knowing I cannot go back

Because that path is forever gone.

I see the light and know it is there

amidst the confusion.

Time will help me get past

the self-imposed angst.

I go back to the lessons learned,

patience and trust.

All will be well somehow.

Reflections

Change can be difficult, fearful, confusing and hard. If we put our trust in God and ask for Spirit's assistance we can move forward onto our new path in life.

What are you stuck in? Are you procrastinating or not moving forward in some way? Are you having an issue with relationships, work, health or otherwise and find that you are afraid to make a decision or take action?

Go within and practice trust and patience and ask Spirit what is holding you back in any way.

To go within means to be quiet and calm yourself until you feel peaceful and loving. During this time ask Spirit's assistance in knowing what is your new path. Be willing to wait and allow Spirit's guidance to come through.

Write down any insights or understandings that come from this.

Section 11

Developing Awareness and Compassion

Section II

Developing Awareness and Compassion

Introduction

Awareness of what is going on is the first step to healing the ego's wounds and spirituality.

Stepping back and becoming an observer of your life and becoming aware of your ego's thoughts and emotions results in seeing your experiences from a higher level rather than just reacting. I refer to this as "Seeing through the Eyes of The Soul". It takes practice but is well worth it. You will become calmer and more loving as you go into your Loving Self and start forgiving others and yourself.

Your Loving Self is that part of you which is peaceful, loving and eternal. Some call it the soul; others call it your higher self and others, your Divine self. I have used these terms interchangeably throughout this book.

You can begin to develop this awareness by first setting an intention every morning, to observe your thoughts and feelings especially when there is upset or disturbance.

Setting an intention means deciding to do or be something. Setting an intention to be an observer of your thoughts, means deciding to be the observer of your life. Intentions are more powerful if there is some action or follow-up.

For example, you might write down your intention in the morning and put the paper up where you will see it during the day. Small steps in the right direction are more effective than huge changes all at once. You might also write about being the observer during the day and what you noticed and learned later in the day.

Especially important is to observe when you experience upset. What triggers feelings of anger, inadequacy or any other negative reaction? When you realize that you are upset about something it is then important to acknowledge your feelings and get in touch with it.

Ask yourself questions such as when did this feeling happen? What is it I am feeling – sadness, anger or something else that does not feel good?

Take the time to explore your feelings instead of reacting to them, denying or ignoring them. When you have done this forgive yourself for your judgments and forgive others that were involved.

Ask yourself what lessons you have learned then come into a state of acceptance by giving up your concerns and bad feelings to God. Yes surrender to God (or whatever word works for you, like Spirit or my higher self.)

Learn to be aware that difficulties are lessons to learn during our lifetime and when we let go of them by acknowledging them and then surrendering them we can heal and be happier and more creative in our lives.

Compassionate Watcher

Like a mischievous little elf he hid and watched

as the old bag lady picked up the fifty dollar bill.

The old woman peered at the money and

blinked her eyes in disbelief.

She then furtively put the cash in a

hidden part of her stained blouse.

Her ruddy cheeks glowed even more brightly

and her step was lighter.

This night she would be fed and could make merry.

This night she would be able to forget.

The watcher had mixed feelings.

Did I help or harm?

But all he could see was the happy smile

and the little dance of joy.

Fleeting though it may be,

she was happy and had more than before

at least for a little while.

God bless her.

Reflections

When we help others it is important to do it through love and without judgment. Everyone has something that they are working through. We are not better than the bag lady in God's eyes.

Do you give to the less fortunate smugly and with a sense of superiority? Can you see the Loving Essence in the bag lady? Do you think you know what is best for people like the bag lady?

Write your thoughts about this poem.

Practice being aware of judgments that you may have of others and let them go.

Practice compassion this week by sending love to all you encounter.

If Only

He sat in bed like a rag doll, thin and worn and in pain.

Every breath sucked in and sucked out.

Needles of pain caught in the diaphragm.

How much longer can he endure?

Slowly, slowly passing on.

One foot here and the other in the grave.

So little time or energy to correct life's mistakes.

The reality is he has no time

to fulfill his dreams or make amends.

The sand slips through the hour glass

so, so very slow and deliberate.

If only -

Reflections

It would be so easy to judge this individual as having failed Life, however if you look at his pain with compassion (not pity) you can see that this is his process of learning his lessons in life.

Perhaps this is also an opportunity for others to express Love and compassion.

Do you know anyone in your life that you feel is a failure?

This week view this person and others with compassion instead of judgment. This means that you don't pity the person but accept them as they are.

Set your intention daily to observe rather than judge.

Write your observations on what you noticed and what you did.

Old and Bitter

She is old and bitter, angry and irritated

at what life has given her.

The aches and pains have become pure agony.

She can't sleep or rest; All that matters is

To lash out and spread the pain

she projects on to those nearby.

They scuttle away and she nods in satisfaction

as if to say, "They don't care."

What she doesn't know is that she drives away

those who would like to help by her angry words.

Her selfish pity only serves to

drown her in her own sorrowful depression.

Reflections

Old age can have challenges that make life difficult. Old age does not mean being grouchy.

This is an opportunity by the older person to practice acceptance and those around them to have the opportunity to be compassionate and not take the outbursts personally.

Can you view older people without judgment or do you pity them?

This week think of older people in your life. Better yet visit them. Practice patience and compassion with them.

If you feel pity then remember that pity means you judge them. Instead be compassionate and set an intention to observe from a higher place.

Reflect on this and write your thoughts down about viewing these people from a higher level. They are doing the best they can and learning lessons as they go. Pray for them and for yourself so that you can be more loving and compassionate.

One Step at a Time

Her mind was a muddled pool of consternation

as she pondered her project.

Little bits of flotsam came up only to sink again.

She couldn't grasp the thread that made sense.

She mulled over her thoughts and stewed for days.

Writing down thoughts helped

and talking to other souls enlightened her.

She finally received clarity and

was ready to move forward one step at a time.

She simply took a breath and began.

Reflections

Sometimes our thoughts become muddled and our ego resists. This occurs when the ego is afraid of success or of learning something new. Overcoming ego's resistance to change takes a conscious choice to allow Spirit to take over.

Do you procrastinate when doing something new or different?

Do you think you are not worthy to do and accomplish new things?

Think about the times that it was difficult for you to start or finish something.

When this occurs ask for Spirit's assistance in getting you through the block.

Meditate or pray, relax and ask for Spirit's assistance.

Become the observer of yourself and notice the feelings that come up. Then forgive yourself for whatever judgments come up. Actually say "I forgive myself for buying into the belief that I am _____. The truth is I am doing the best I can. "

Then set your intention to move on.

Take a deep breath and start.

Precipice of Change

I look down the cliff with fear

and wait until I'm ready.

Overwhelmed with excitement

I still hesitate to take the first step.

Am I ready? Is this the time?

I don't know enough about the future.

Anticipation thrills me and

beckons me like a lover.

I tremble and gasp

then ask Spirit to assist me

as I take the leap

to face the unknown and untried

the challenge of the new.

The more I trust and surrender

the more beauty and grace unfolds me.

The adventure of life is a

never ending joy of changing experiences.

Reflections

We are constantly experiencing changes as we grow and learn life's lessons. These changes can be unsettling but the truth is that we are Spirit which never changes. The Ego is where we experience change. When we learn to trust our Spiritual self then life can be joyous no matter what is going on.

How do you handle change in your life?

In your journal write about how you handle change in your life.

Start with setting an intention to surrender to change as God's will.

Next, ask for Spirit's assistance in accepting life's changes with ease and grace.

Then you can reframe the challenges of life's unknown as opportunities to enjoy new things. Reframing means that you look at something (like your resistance to change) and decide to look at it in a more positive way, for example as an opportunity or challenge.

Change can then become something to enjoy.

Write about this process and how it affected you.

Stretching

As I stretched into my new self

the fit was tight and uncomfortable.

There was no taking off the new suit

I soon found out.

No going backward, only forward.

So I looked for the light and

joyously wriggled into a new space.

Ahhh, I did it!

I emerged as more than before

and found it wonderful and brand new.

Thank you Spirit for the challenge

and the opportunity.

Reflections

Stretching and growing can be uncomfortable as we change our way of being and thinking.

Once we make the commitment to change and grow we cannot go back. Trying to go back will only cause pain and slow down the change. At this point it is best to surrender to God's will and allow yourself to change or move on. Once you get through the process you will feel better and your self-esteem will improve.

Have you ever made a commitment to grow and felt uncomfortable during the process?

Is there a challenge in your life that you are struggling with?

Have you acknowledged your feelings and finally did you surrender to God?

Write about a current situation or one from the past where you dealt with changes and growth.

Write about how you handled it and how you felt after.

The Winner

Driving home a point he shook his fist.

Face flushed with excitement trying

to convince his opponent the truth

of his words as his voice rose higher and higher.

Like a fencing match they both scored points.

Who was the real winner?

In the end nobody cared.

Reflections

Reacting with anger to an angry person accomplishes nothing but hurt feelings. Nobody wins and there is damage to the relationship. You can train yourself to see things through the eyes of your Soul and respond to others with Love.

Do you automatically react to a person who is yelling at you? Can you step back and look at the situation from a higher level?

This week set an intention to take on the role of observer as much as possible. Don't react or judge just observe. You can then think calmly and respond but continue to observe your response.

This is a difficult practice but gets easier with time.

Write about this and what you learned or noticed.

Too Hurt For Love

She lashed out in fury

because she felt lost and unappreciated.

Her lesson was about being unheard and unloved.

Anything else was brushed aside as irrelevant.

She was too hurt, too wounded, the ultimate victim.

She cried out, "Don't you see what you did and what you are?

When what she meant was, "I'm afraid, please comfort me."

Her outward attack reflected her inner disturbance.

Reality was, we all do the best we can.

The answer is the loving inside her and all of us.

Reflections

This poem talks about someone who is hurt and lashes out in a verbal attack.

The first response by many people would to respond in kind. Attacking back does no good and can escalate the situation. Instead if you are faced with this kind of verbal attack send Love until you are in control and the attacker calms down. Make a choice to listen rather than respond and don't take things personally.

Practice listening and your relationships will very likely improve.

Have you been in such a situation and ended up arguing back? Did things improve or get worse when you got upset?

Write in your journal about someone who pushes your buttons and makes you angry.

If you have the opportunity to meet this person again prepare yourself by meditating and calming yourself before the encounter. Set an intention to remain calm and instead of reacting with anger, ask, "What do you want me to hear?" Decide that you will be ready to listen instead of being defensive.

Write about your experiences after listening compassionately.

Unworthy of Love

She rode the darkness to the depths of despair

'til she could go no further.

Then she sat there and dwelt in the sadness

feeling unworthy of love.

Each time she struggled up

through the muck then

was pulled down once more.

The cycle repeated again and again.

Where is the Love?

Where is the joy?

Finally with each repetition

she began to break the surface

and then realized that she had been stuck

in the mire of deception.

The lesson learned was that the strength

was within all along.

Love was inside and

melted the gloom and doom

when she forgave the unworthy thoughts

that opened her to the glory of her own soul.

Reflections

This poem is about depression; a state of sadness. Extreme depression is sadness that is very deep, long lasting and often life threatening. It may require professional help if it persists. The ego holds on to this sadness until it is looked at and forgiven. Forgiveness uncovers the love that exists within each one of us.

How do you deal with sadness? What is really bothering you?

Write in your journal about what this poem means to you.

Allow any sadness to surface and ask to let go and surrender it to God/Spirit.

Self forgiveness in this case is very important. Forgive yourself by saying, "I forgive myself for judging myself as (worthless, or whatever fits)"

Then forgive any people involved.

Write about your experience.

If you are not sad reflect on how you dealt with it in the past and thank God for your happiness today.

Section III

Go Within

Section III

Go Within

Introduction

Our Loving Essence also known as our Soul and the part of us that is loving and eternal, is accessible to us all.

I recommend starting a program of Spiritual practices such as meditation, prayer and forgiveness. Practice letting go and surrender to God, who is pure love, especially when experiencing a disturbance.

To meditate start with silence or very soothing music. Make yourself comfortable and relaxed. There are different techniques for meditation but the one that works best for me is to concentrate on my breath and let thoughts float by as they come up. I then focus on the feeling of love. Start with 5 minutes once or twice a day than gradually increase to 15 minutes or more. After practicing this consistently you will get better at letting go of your thoughts and feeling the peace and love of your Divine Essence.

Prayer works well also, especially when surrendering yourself to God's will. Forgiveness as a Spiritual practice helps one heal and become calmer and loving.

Everyday ask how and who can I forgive today? This helps to let go of judgments and surrender.

Finally another way to access Spirit is to be in nature and appreciate the beauty all around us. Calmly and quietly feeling the beauty of nature can bring us in touch with the loving inside.

Discovering Herself

It felt like its own life force in her chest

was about to birth itself.

The pressure in her heart area grew

until the light burst through

with an amazing yet gentle force.

Such joy, such peace, such bliss!

Is this what they call Love?

The being before her said,

You have simply uncovered the

True Divine Being that you are.

Love heals all, go within for sustenance

for all else is only a temporary illusion.

Reflections

In this poem the person experiences Love and joy in such a blissful way that Light seems to shine from her heart area. A being appears to explain that Love heals all.

Is this an angel or relative who has passed over? Is there someone who looks over you? What is your real nature? Is Love within?

To get better at going within practice going within this week using one of the techniques I mentioned in the introduction to this section. Practice feeling the loving. Start the process by being quiet and letting go of thoughts. Later reflect on the poem and ask yourself what this means to you.

You may wish to write your thoughts and review them during the week.

Home

The rain stopped and the beacon of light

shone brightly in the dark night,

a reminder to all that love was still there.

Hope lingered in the mist

that one could still find home.

Home, yes home was there all along.

Such joy, such comfort when the realization sunk in

and warmed the hearts of all who sought peace.

Reflections

For most of us home is that place of refuge and love. We feel safe and loved in our home. This comfort has always been there and is available whenever you need it. God is our home and resides within.

What does the term home mean to you? Is it a place of comfort and reassurance? If for some reason it is not a place of comfort, what is a place of comfort for you?

This week through meditation, prayer or the forgiveness exercise you can practice going "home".

You might want to start this process by being silent then move into your loving essence.

If you wish write down your thoughts and feelings.

Musical Upliftment

The music lifts me like the ocean swells gently

in rhythms soft and caring.

The tones touch me in chakra points

which stir me to my depths.

I close my eyes and soar

into eternity and back.

I find a peaceful bliss as I let

myself surrender to undulating

notes and pitter patters.

It's as if I'm swirling in love and peace.

I am safe and loved in the womb of

sound encircling me.

Reflections

Music can be soothing or energizing. It can also bring your energy down. Music can be calming and centering or it can do just the opposite. Realizing this and choosing appropriate music helps one focus on feelings of peace, Love and harmony.

What kind of music is soothing and calming to you?

What kind of music is energizing in a positive way?

What kind of music brings your energy down?

Think about what music soothes you, energizes you or brings you down.

Write about this and if you find it helpful start to use music to uplift you in positive ways only.

Peace Begins With Me

Peace begins with me.

I go inside and feel the stillness.

The calm washes over me so gently.

I feel the harmony of all life and I can face the world.

As I encounter discord I see the peace

in between the vibrations.

Anger, fear, hatred, fear are all opposites

of love, joy and courage.

I look for what I want to find

and I find it there, everywhere,

Peace.

Reflections

When we become more aware of the stillness inside we can go there for replenishment. Peace is within even when there are problems all around us.

What disturbances appear in your life? Are they causing you upset?

You can practice going within by meditation, prayer and the other spiritual practices covered in the chapter introduction.

If you go within and make a conscious choice to see the lesson and the good in your life you will uplift the whole planet with the energy of Peace and Love.

Peace Is There

Peace is there and fear is gone.

Peace is there and anger fades away.

Goodness is in all of us if we choose to find it.

Love is the way to acceptance of the infinite.

It is a choice we make that goes beyond mind,

body, emotions and into spirit.

Reflections

Peace which is an aspect of Love is in all of us. By being silent and going within we can tap into this calming bliss. If we spend time dwelling with Spirit, we can let go of fear. Ways to do this are yoga, meditation, prayer and spending time in nature. This kind of spiritual practice helps calm you so that you can go about your day in a peaceful way.

How can you be peaceful even when in the midst of chaos?

This week make a conscious choice to nourish yourself alone in silence. Let go of distractions and focus on the peace.

Don't worry if you still have thoughts coming in. Let them float by as you clear your mind. Start with 5 minutes a day than increase gradually until you can do 15 to 20 minutes or more.

Set an intention to do this every day.

If you like write in your journal about going within and experiencing more peace in your life.

Tired

Her hand felt like a lead weight,

eyes sore and tired like burning goals.

All she wanted was sleep

that wonderful state of the netherland

between dreaming and waking where whispers

of light and truths come in all shapes and forms.

Things to tell to help if one heeds.

She yawned and pressed on.

Just a little and she would be done.

Then time to rest.

Reflections

The natural rhythms of life require rest. In fact sleep is when we renew ourselves and keep in touch with spirit. Insights and answers can come to us in our sleep.

If we ask spirit each night to answer a question or resolve a problem the answer will come. In the morning write down the first thing that you remember. This might not make sense at first but review your writings every few days and see if you understand the messages given to you by Spirit. Best results occur if you do this for a month or more. This gives time for patterns and insights to appear.

Did you ever wake up with an insight to a problem? Did you ever wake up and wonder what your dream was about?

For a week or more set an intention at bedtime to get answers regarding a problem or concern you have.

Keep a notepad by your bed and write down whatever you remember dreaming about.

Review what you wrote down frequently to understand the message.

Section IV

Awe, Wonder, Gratitude

Section IV

Awe, Wonder, Gratitude

Introduction

I find that developing an attitude of gratitude and wonder helps me experience the Loving in me which is my soul.

There are practices which can assist in this development. One is to start each day by writing down 5 to 10 things for which you are grateful. This may be hard at first but with practice you will get better at this process. You can start with "I am grateful to be alive", "I am grateful for the nice weather". This practice puts you in a start of loving appreciation which is a feeling of awe and wonder.

Awe and wonder can also be cultivated by setting time aside to look at beauty such as a perfect flower, art, perfectly crafted items we use every day (such as furniture) or even listening to the sound of beautiful music. As the old saying goes "take time to smell the coffee".

Awe, wonder and gratitude helps each of us view life from a higher level, in other words through the eyes of the soul. We can see the connection we have with others and all of creation. We can understand others and accept their process of healing even if they are directing their upset at us. We can see the beauty, wonder of nature and the Loving Essence in people.

The Loving Essence which is our Spiritual self, lives in this glorious state at all times. Tapping into this source of Loving allows us all to experience life to the fullest.

Love's Choice

When the choice is Love, one

can come to profound freedom and peace.

This is the journey to Godliness.

It's possible to soar on spirit's wings like the eagle and see

that we are all one beautiful expression of the Divine.

Over the earth and the seas, the stars, all things,

and people are one fabulous ecstasy of love.

When I look at creation this way how can I not

see exquisite Goodness.

Reflections

So often we look at what we perceive as negative. We make judgments such as the world is crazy, people are mean, or the environment is dirty. If we practice seeing the world in awe, wonder and with gratitude then we see that everything good or bad has a purpose to help each of us grow in Love. Spending time in nature and allowing oneself to experience the beauty and perfection of all life is a way to see through the eyes of the soul.

Have you ever experienced awe and wonder?

Have you ever felt gratitude fully and with great appreciation?

How does being in a state of awe, wonder and gratitude feel?

It is suggested that every day for a week or more practice being in the state of awe and wonder. Marvel at how nature operates. Look at a plant and feel the magnificence of all life. Look at nature where you live and notice how perfect and beautiful it is.

Writing about your experiences of being in the state of awe, wonder and gratitude will help you continue to be in this beautiful state.

Ready for the Next Step

Above we saw a blue grey canopy

filled with glorious twinkling lights.

The air carried a warm fragrance

that tingled the nose.

I felt on the verge of marvelous new adventures,

unknown but there nevertheless.

My tummy flip flops in anticipation and

I am ready to take the next leap of faith,

I take my love by the hand and we hold our breath

as we leap and tumble with exhilaration.

Life is good. Life is wonderful.

God leads me to further wonders

that I am only beginning to see.

Reflections

Being grateful and in a state of wonder helps us see beauty and Love everywhere. When we look at our new steps in life as adventures instead of worrying about exactly how things will turn out, we allow ourselves to experience life with joy.

Do you agonize over new things or changes in your life?

Do you want to know exactly how things in your life will happen?

Start every day with gratitude. Thank God for even the smallest things.

Write at least 5 things that you are grateful for.

Then think about these blessings and allow wonder and joy to fill your life.

Spring Is Here

There is a sense of change in the air.

Spring is here.

I feel the emanations everywhere.

Time to hug those so dear.

The promise of newness and life

is sure to appear.

The ageless cycle continues its rhythm,

a power so true and clear.

Reflections

Spring is a time of newness and hope. There is a sense of rebirth and starting over again to produce God's creation.

Similar things happen in our lives as we go through different stages. We go from being a child to a young adult then from a young adult to a middle aged one and so on. Each stage is a renewing of ourselves and starting over as a different person. Hopefully we have learned from the past and can move on gracefully.

Can you relate Spring to your life?

Does the sense of rebirth and starting over frighten you or exhilarate you?

Meditate on the feeling of hope and newness. After your meditation write down what new things you would like to accomplish in the next 6 months to a year.

Allow yourself to feel grateful for new opportunities.

Too Precious

Don't hold back.

You are too precious to waste a drop

of your gracious essence on fear.

Everyone wants a taste of your glory.

Hiding yourself is only selfish.

Lead the way and connect.

Your Spirit lights us all with Love.

Such wonder uncloaks itself if you

only allow your true self

to come out and play.

Reflections

We are all children of God. This preciousness is a wonder. We are here to live our life's purpose which is to Love oneself and all others. When we hide our talents and gifts we are not appreciating what God has given us and we are not sharing our preciousness with the world.

When you are grateful for your gifts and use them for the glorious expression of the Divine then Love connects you to your purpose.

Do you downplay your gifts?

Have you really thought about what you have been blessed with?

Can you see how the world needs you to express your talents and gifts?

Take time to be grateful for the gifts you have. Be grateful for your life and the opportunity to express yourself with love.

List your talents, assets and gifts that you are blessed to have.

Then sit and thank God for being who you are.

What is Peace Like

Peace is like soft cotton

that I like to pat down.

Peace is the airy freshness

of a summer breeze.

Peace is the warmth of

the sun on my face.

Peace is comfort, love and joy.

Peace is a freedom I have

finally found possible.

Reflections

Peace is an experience of Love and joy. We sometimes don't allow ourselves to feel it because the ego says we can't or shouldn't. Overcoming the fear in our lives means we are accepting God.

How does it feel to be at peace with yourself and all life?

Meditate on the quality of peace. Feel the softness and comfort of Peace. Go within and achieve the freedom of peace. Let go of all fear.

Do this peace meditation for a week or so.

After a week ask yourself if you are overall more peaceful.

Wonder

I am caught in the air of wonder,

fresh and flowery and invigorating.

So much to see and do and experience.

I close my eyes in delicious expectancy.

It is glorious to be alive today.

I am grateful to still breathe this precious life.

Oh, another chance to explore God's gifts today!

Reflections

Being in the state of wonder, awe and gratitude is an experience of the Soul. When you feel in wonder then you experience the Love of Spirit. Your actions will be more compassionate and you also unleash your own personal creativity.

When you practice gratitude you will become more aware of your blessings and more accepting of life's challenges.

Wonder awe and gratitude may take practice but will be worth it as you learn to accept and appreciate life as a gift.

How does it feel to be in a state of wonder?

How does it feel to have an attitude of gratitude?

Every day write 5 things that you are grateful for.

Then feel the gratitude and wonder of life wash over you.

Do this every day for a week or more and it will become easier and easier to appreciate life's lessons even difficult ones.

Section V

Connection to All Creation

Section V

Connection to all Creation

Introduction

Today's world teaches us that we are separate from other people, other countries, and other creatures. It teaches that we are independent and that competition is the way to success and happiness. We hear phrases such as "Dog eat dog" which indicates a consciousness where there is never enough, we have to fight to survive and selfishness is the rule of the day. This awareness is even reflected in terms of nationalism and patriotism which means we justify and focus on only our own wants and needs.

I believe we are not only citizens of our countries but also of the world and even of the universe. When we expand our thinking (consciousness) we take our personal perspectives aside and look at the whole picture. This means we realize our connection with all creation.

As said before when you become the Observer of your life you can see yourself and others from a higher level. Remember that your ego wants you to see the world from its limited perspective. Just imagine going up above the world and look at yourself and your surroundings, then go further up into outer space and look at the earth. How beautiful the earth looks and you can't even see the tiny little humans on it let alone, the plants, animals, buildings and so on. Now go further out into the universe and you will not see the earth as it is but merely as a spec. Do your judgments, differences and upsets seem important now? Do you feel separate now or a part of the whole universe?

When a person enters the room can you feel the energy of the person? Do you feel good or do you sense agitation or some other feeling? Our connection to others means we are affected by them and they are influenced by each of us. We are not always aware of this but if we pay attention and intentionally feel the other person's energy we can sense many things about them. We can then realize their influence on us. In turn our attitude affects those around you. Knowing each one of us affects others even without speaking is a sacred duty to be loving and non-judgmental of others.

When we are in nature it is possible to sense the Divine energy present. It is calming and refreshing. We can then realize our connection to nature and in turn strive to preserve it. The fact is nature sustains us by giving us clean air, water and food so it is important to realize this connection and protect our environment.

Autumn

It flows in quietly, brushing by ever so softly.

Autumn swept through the hills like the ebb and flow of the tide.

As the wind picked up she held her coat tightly and shivered.

Currents of cool and warm, then cold came

as a cacophony of temperatures on the wind.

She looked forward to the sleep of winter

A time to heal and repair.

Then the cycle begins again with for the newness of Spring.

Reflections

We are all part of nature. Indeed we are part of the Divine order.

Does this make you think of the eternal rhythms of life?

Do you think all life has a purpose?

Reflect on this and determine what you know is your connection to God and all life.

Write down your thoughts and set your intention to observe nature's rhythms for the next week.

Desert Splendor

A mild breeze tickled the leaves.

Some left their higher perch

and floated softly to the ground,

almost in whispers.

Peace and an infinite knowing

of ancient truths filled one with wonder,

the wonder of God.

There was a certain reverence felt

as one looked across the canyons and mountains.

Everything was fresh and new,

yet an old wisdom orchestrated the beauty;

a symphony of color,

some soft and muted,

others bright and dazzling,

some earthy and warm.

One felt part of the splendor

and united in the spirit of the land.

The same energy,

the same cosmic vibration

touched us all

and left us forever changed.

Reflections

When quiet reflective time is spent in nature, a sense of wonder develops and brings us closer to Spirit.

Have you ever spent time observing and feeling nature?

How does this make you feel?

Do you feel peaceful and in awe?

Do you feel a power bigger than yourself?

Be the observer this week and notice nature around you. Notice the color, texture, smells of nature and how this makes you feel.

Write down your feelings about this.

Growth

The flower blooms in all

its wondrous glory.

The caterpillar will metamorphose into

the butterfly that flutters away.

All these things come in their own time sure and true.

The evolution of human consciousness

moves at an increasing pace.

Though some can only see the preceding turmoil,

the seedlings are planted and soon to wave

like grass in the breeze,

as the new knowledge of light takes hold

and a new way of being comes about.

Reflections

We are still growing and evolving as humans. Nature has its own changes and periods of growth. This in turn means that just as nature goes through its cycles of growth and decay, so does mankind. There is change in the air, often preceded by disasters but the growth in human consciousness is steady and unalterable.

Change and growth begins with one individual at a time. As you grow in awareness, all of mankind grows too.

Can you think of a situation where you changed and grew?

Did people around you change too?

Practice <u>being</u> Love, kindness, forgiveness and compassion.

Every day for at least a week start with the intention of <u>being</u> one of these states of consciousness. For example you can start with the intention that today I am going to be Love. Tell yourself "Everything I do will be from a place of Love". Also you can tell yourself "I radiate Love".

Notice how people react to you. Practice on the other traits one or two days each and notice how people are around you.

You may wish to write about this in your journal and what you discovered.

Palm Springs Sunset

Palm Trees in the sun shimmered and shook in the wind.

The warm sun sparkled but

Fall's cool fingers stroked the fronds of the trees.

The hazy mountain in the background

suddenly eclipsed the area

in a slithering darkness as the cold shadow

drew its breath along the still earth.

Night came suddenly as it does this time of year

but only because rest is needed for what is to come.

Reflections

Palm Springs is nestled in between mountains. During winter when nightfall comes earlier than any other time of year the mountains block the sun as it goes down each evening resulting in the darkness coming suddenly. There is another lesson from nature here. There are times in our lives when darkness seems to fall over us. It can happen suddenly and cause great distress. Just remember that this is a time for rest and an acknowledgement that the darkness is not necessarily bad but rather a time to assess the situation and learn from our mistakes.

Has there been a time when things went badly and later when looking back you realized that the experience was necessary for you to grow?

Are you going through such a time in the present time?

Reflect on current or former bad experiences. Think about how to look at the situation as a learning experience. On former bad experiences, for example, you may now look on them as a gift because you learned some valuable lesson.

If going through a tough time currently see what limiting beliefs may be involved.

Determine if these beliefs are still valid.

Forgive yourself for these beliefs and forgive anyone else who you might believe is involved.

Finally give up the darkness in your life to God.

Planetary Awakening

There is a stirring undercurrent of thought.

What if love could solve all our problems?

No, That can't be, that's never been the answer.

Man is too weak, too corrupt, too bad!

Just look at how history repeats itself.

War, violence, anger, hate, always prevailed.

Where is the love then?

The truth is that these are only

temporary finite things put in our way.

Divinity is more wondrous in Its Own Wisdom.

Love is here, always was, forever and ever,

and can only be found when we awaken to it

with true acceptance.

Reflections

People are beginning to realize that all the problems and poor choices made by mankind can be resolved by Love. This happens one person at a time but the momentum is building.

As people realize that the answer to solving the world's problems is collaboration rather than competition, and love not repression or violence, then this new way of thinking and being will create harmony in the world.

Does it seem that history keeps repeating itself?

Is there more violence today? Is it possible to have a civilization that is in harmony with the Divine order of things?

In fact is there Love, Peace and harmony already, it we just realize it's there?

Reflect on these questions and write in your journal what you think about whether things are better or worse today.

Also think about the good things that people do such as small kindnesses and generosity.

Summer's End

The Divine's hot breath hit our faces

as we flew over the water.

The crystal blue water was cool,

almost icy as we dipped in the healing liquid.

Young and old people were everywhere;

pumping hormones of the young

seen in their tanned toned bodies.

Families enjoying the last days of summer

only to start the cycle again next season.

Reflections

We are all connected to each other. Young and old people are living the cycles of nature learning different lessons appropriate to their age. Young people are learning rapidly and developing who they are destined to be. Adults are often focused on success and child rearing. In later years it is common for people to reflect on what is the meaning of their life.

What stage of life are you in now?

Can you see a common theme regarding what is important to you now?

Imagine different times in your life and how you felt and what you learned.

Now progress through to old age. Think about what you will learn in your later years.

Be grateful for the opportunities in all phases of your life.

This Moment is Special

I look to the future with glorious expectancy.

I look to the past, grateful for it lessons.

I steep in the beauty of the now,

blessed, here, this moment,

so peaceful and happy to be alive.

Nature in all its splendor

greets me as the sun

brushes my face with warmth.

All around me is alive with beauty

and surrounds me with love.

I glow brighter and brighter until my heart bursts

with the fire of Divinity.

Color is so vivid, so clear.

This moment is special.

I am one with nature,

one with all,

one with God.

Reflections

Nature connects us to Spirit in very powerful way. When in nature it is possible to experience the colors more vividly and feel incredible joy.

Can you feel the connection with God when you are alone in nature?

What do you notice when you let go of all your cares and concentrate on the beauty of God's creation?

Spend time outdoors and practice becoming one with nature. Notice how alive and beautiful nature is.

Appreciate nature's beauty and experience the essence of never ending Divinity. Soak in this moment with great appreciation. Even the desert has its own beauty.

Remember this moment by writing down your feelings so that later you can re-read about your connection with nature and God.

The Search

She searched for her own kind in the multitude

of faces she came across.

All she saw was greed and anger and pride.

She felt out of place, different somehow

even though she looked the same.

What she longed for was to talk to someone who

understood that what really mattered was

not to be stronger, better, richer or prettier

but only to be at peace with whatever it was

that was the essence of you and me.

Color, size, shape, riches or power

did not make the difference, only the light,

the beauty that glowed from within.

Indeed knowing this is what she looked for

so that she could share her vision and

know that she was understood.

Reflections

Many people are searching for meaning while their ego tells them that they are separate from others.

The truth is we are all exactly where we are meant to be – learning as we go in this world. The answer to this dilemma is to be authentic and talk about how we feel even if we feel vulnerable. It may surprise you how others will accept you.

Are you on a quest for spiritual growth?

Do you feel alone in this endeavor?

What does this mean to you?

Consider starting a study group discussing spiritual concepts such as non-judgment, compassion, and forgiveness.

Practice being the observer of your own behavior and that of others.

When There are No Secrets

People touch each other and don't know it

as drops in the pond radiate outward.

We are all affected by thoughts both spoken or silent.

If we knew the effects, would we change?

This is the awareness that can alter

our perceptions.

When we know and understand

our thoughts and words on another and

they know theirs on us,

then there are no secrets.

Only when we are all exposed

and vulnerable will honesty prevail.

It is then that Love can serve to uplift us all.

Reflections

We are all connected in Spirit. Often we don't know it, but we sense the emotions that others bring into the room.

Have you ever noticed the energy that people bring into the room?

Is it happy, sad, joyful or angry?

This week focus on sensing the energy that people bring into the room.

Also focus on your own feelings and thoughts and what effect they have on others.

Test your unspoken effect on others by sending Love to an individual and notice the reaction.

Praise

"Leona's work touches the soul by artfully illustrating Spiritual concepts. She provides the opportunity to reflect on and practice these concepts by guiding the reader to go within and find the Love in us all." ~ Will Sherwood, CEO, The Sherwood Group

"Leona's vast array of poetry is at once insightful, as it is artistic and aesthetic. You will feel colorful emotions that are subtly described in her passages. This is a must read." ~ Brenda Fenner, Senior Buyer

" It is has been my experience that whenever I am searching for answers to situations I encounter on my life's journey, I am led within. Here, I can connect with the deeper, inner parts of myself to find solutions. In reading Leona's poetic expressions, it appears that she, too, frequently journeys within to find that Divine, tranquil part of herself to connect with. Her poems speak to my heart and help me move forward in my many roles that 'Stretch me into my new self." ~ Ann Hill, Businesswoman, Professional Speaker, Co-contributor "The 'G' Spot", the ecstasy of life through GRATITUDE" book.

"Leona's spiritual insights into life's many twists and turns goes beyond what you see in the moment. Her insight goes to the core of a bigger picture and imparts grace to our human experience, which is reflected into the heart of her poems." ~ Sharone Strohm , Entrepreneur, Writer, Spiritual Coach

"Leona's poems take the reader on an introspective journey towards love and acceptance of being. I recommend it to anyone searching for inner peace and understanding." ~Xavier Melanson-Fernandez, Environmental Scientist.

104

www.ingramcontent.com/pod-product-compliance
Lightning Source LLC
Chambersburg PA
CBHW071609040426
42452CB00008B/1297